# The Call: When Leaders Say Yes

By: Tamara Simmons

ISBN 979-8-88616-241-7 (paperback)
ISBN 979-8-88616-242-4 (digital)



Christian Faith Publishing
832 Park Avenue
Meadville, PA 16335
www.christianfaithpublishing.com

Printed in the United States of America

# Preface

I have come to learn that God is a master planner. As I reminisce over my life and the phases I have journeyed through thus far, I can say I am truly grateful. All things are working together for my good.

For approximately four years, this book has only been a seed planted in my mind. Time and life experiences were the soil that gave this seed the necessary nutrients it needed to grow. What sprung from that soil was the fruit that blossomed into this: *The Call: When Leaders Say Yes*.

To each reader, I am hopeful you are blessed by this short presentation.

# Acknowledgment

I would like to mention some amazing people in my life. To my husband and best friend, Trevor Simmons, who made writing this book a topic every day. You are a key and a gift to my existence. Thank you, sir. I love you.

To my sister, Brittney Precious Cox. Thank you for always being there for me, even when I was too busy to be there for you. To my brother Delano and biggest supporter, thank you. To my mom, thank you for believing in me always. To my entire family, thank you so much. There were so many family events I missed, so many calls I was unable to return in a timely manner. Your love and support remain consistent.

Thank you, Broken in Worship ministries, for your love and unfailing support always.

# CONTENTS

# CHAPTER 1

# Acknowledging the Call

If you are like me, you probably grew up watching the infamous Trinity Broadcasting Network (TBN). Back then, in my eyes, what I saw was the greatest thing ever. I often recall sitting in front of the television screen and being astounded watching hands laid on persons, and they would be slain or information about their lives revealed to them by strangers.

I really didn't fully understand the depth of what was going on. It was intriguing, and I was drawn.

In this current time and era, it appears that leadership, the five-fold ministry title (a minister in charge of a Christian church or congregation), is desired among many.

If the truth is told, some of us were enamored by the thought of being used by God and not with God himself. I believe this was the case for some of us because on the onset, we didn't understand that being used by God would require sacrifice and its fair share of responsibility. We saw someone we admired doing great things. It is quite easy to be enticed by the prize and not comprehend the price that must be paid.

To gain this prize, one must say yes to the toughest question they will ever have to answer: "Will *you go?*" To the naked eye, this three-worded question appears simple, but to anyone that had to agree to disrupt their current course, to follow the *will* of *God*, they understand perfectly the meaning of these words.

An anonymous author penned, "The one who takes responsibility is leading." The one who influences others is leading. The one who makes a difference is leading. The wisdom in this thought is that leadership qualities can be attributed to anyone in a moment.

There is a difference between leading for a brief moment and rising to the call of a leader for a time span of years or decades. In case you are asking what is the difference, if a fire takes place in the neighborhood there may be some that began thinking quickly to save lives. They assisted to retrieve children and out fires. This is a very heroic feature but this moment won't happen every day. In contrast, there maybe a gentleman in his community that became burden by decisions of young men in his community. He decided to devote his time to character and academic development in hopes their futures will be successful. He does this for the next twenty-five years. In both instances, all persons are leaders but the latter has risen to the call of a leader for a life time or a longer time.

As you read this, you can exhale. You just found the reason why the light in your passion will not go out. It's simply because you have not only decided to lead in a moment. You made the onerous decision to say yes to become a leader beyond just a moment but for every single moment you are needed. This would mean guiding a people, taking responsibility for the good and the bad moments, and putting the pieces back together after life disassembles what you have built.

It is important to know that becoming an effective leader is a lifelong journey. There is no end to this accomplishment. There will always be something new to learn or an area you can improve in. When you embrace this, you have won half the battle.

When answering the call to be an effective leader, you must commit time, curiosity, and study to answering the following four questions:

- What is my leadership style?
- Who will I lead?
- Where and for what specific purpose am I leading?

It is important to know or learn the type of leader you are. There are some attributes that will develop during the journey. Each of us has an innate ability to lead. Therefore, there is an existing leadership culture in you. During my quest to find these answers for myself, I learned that there are many ways one can lead. I want to share nine of them with you. As you read, try to find which one is your leadership style.

1. Autocratic leadership

    This is one of the strictest types. This kind of leader tends to have complete control over the decision-making process. This leadership style can be effective when decision-making is urgent or workmanship is routine.

2. Bureaucratic leadership

    This leadership style is not as strict as the aforementioned. However, this type of leader strictly enforces rules of an hierarchy.

3. Charismatic leadership

    This type of leader is very infectious. They are likable. This gives them great success in their endeavors.

4. Democratic leadership

    This style of leadership welcomes those under their authority to assist in decision-making.

5. Laissez-faire leadership

    This kind of leader leads with a hands-off approach. They allow those working with them to assume responsibility for decision-making. However, they do set standards and monitor performance.

6. Servant leadership

    This type of leader shares power and decision-making with subordinates and leads the organization according to the interest of the team.

7. Situational leadership

    Possessing a range of leadership styles to meet the need of different times and situations.
8. Transactional leader

    This type of leaders expresses gratitude very often and in a tangible way by giving gifts and rewards to those working with them.
9. Transformational leadership

    This type of leader is quite similar to charismatic leaders. However, their energy and likable personality are even more infectious. This builds confidence, and accountability causes a greater positive effect on the organization.

All these types outline to us specific ways that a leader carries out their assignment. If a leader has a clear understanding of how they lead, they can better plan and develop their leadership strategies.

When you have answered the how, you then focus on the who or the what. Who have you been called to lead?

It is pertinent that we all seek and receive the answers to the above questions. The answers are the foundation of serving with precision and relevant strategy.

To this end, I would like to call our attention to a specific class of leaders we refer to as pastoral leaders.

These are men and women chosen by God to carry out an assignment within the earth. That will include protecting, teaching, guiding, and imparting into the lives of a set of people for the purpose of building up the Body of Christ.

It has been my absolute honor to have been trusted to author this book. I am grateful to you for sharing this experience with me.

I clearly remember how terrified I was when answering this call. I looked for materials to answer the specific topics mentioned in the book but to no avail.

If you are a lead pastor, a person trying to understand their pastoral leader, or working on a team in your local church, I feel this book will be a blessing to you whether you are mastering or struggling in your call, there will be days when you will need answers, and there will be days you will give them.

I encourage you to remain steadfast. You have been called to the kingdom for such a time as this!

C HAPTER 2

# Transitioning into Leadership

Becoming this kind of leader is more than a career choice. It is a call. One of the hardest things about this call is, often times, we are viewed as superheroes and sheroes. Many of us have believed this at one time or another ourselves.

But then suddenly, life made us painfully aware of the reality; we are human. We must embrace the truth that we cannot save everyone, we cannot please everyone, we cannot be everywhere, *and* we won't have all the answers.

It is only the splendor of God, the one who has called us, that has performed such a wondrous thing. That despite the abovementioned being true, it is also true that the men and women of God in the body of Christ is not just a group of random people who happened to be gifted or propitious, but we are his elect and have been called in such a time because the need for us have arrived.

Leaders, God chose you for a purpose. You possess something unique that another leader does not have. What another leader does not possess is why you are needed right now.

Anyone can possess leadership attributes. However, effective leadership in the Body of Christ lies within your ability to agree and comply with the will of God.

You may be asking the following question: After I say yes to follow God's will, what's next?

6

Pastoral leaders will experience two very important phases within their lives:

1. The call (the time when you knew this is what God wanted you to do)
2. The resources to carry out the call (for each leader, this can be different)

God will equip you to do what he has called you to do. These resources are not always tangible things, like a building or lots of money. Many times, it is the life lessons to make us ready as individuals for an assignment such as this.

The role of a pastor or fivefold ministry leader is a resource in itself designed by God to meet needs and become solutions in the Body of Christ.

> So he gave some apostles, and some prophets, and some evangelists, and some pastors and teachers for the perfecting of the saints. (Ephesians 4:11 KJV)

The word *perfect* or *perfection* is synonymous with excellence. Your role in the Body of Christ is to serve those in your care to not just make them better but make them excellent.

When having to do this with so many different personalities, this can become one of the most disconcerting and challenging things ever.

In order to carry out this job effectively, we are required to first possess what we are called to impart.

The implication then is that once the call of God is answered, we are now on a quest to become equipped ourselves.

Now that you know your call, have you learned your call? I know you are watching videos or reading books as you are right now. But have you learned your specific call? Have you found your specificity? That is very important.

I encourage you to not only become acquainted with what there is to learn about the daily operations of a church ministry but also learn about why God stopped your career, took you from a life of sin, and defied the odds just to set you on this course.

God did not do that to employ another pastor. He wanted *you* and all the unique things in your makeup that will change lives in your own special way.

Therefore, the teacher must agree to become a student forever. Submitting to the classroom for the rest of our lives will guarantee the ability to effectively carry out our assignment from season to season.

Every leader possesses unique qualities that others may not. As said earlier, this is one of the reasons you have been chosen: "You meet a need."

Some of these distinctive qualities can range from, but is not limited to, a preaching style, a traumatic experience. Yes, you read it correctly. Your traumatic experience can be a unique quality, a short-coming (handicap), a gift of wisdom, and so much more.

If God has called you to carry out this assignment at this time or if you have already begun, know that the kingdom has need of *you* now. You may consider your unique qualities as insignificant. But to the people God has assigned to flourish from your impartation, it is the prerequisite to their excellence.

In 2012, I had yet another encounter that has changed my life forever. It was a conversation between my husband and me. He said to me, "The Lord has said to him that he and I would pastor a church."

Dumbfounded and afraid all at the same time, I told him, "This could not be so." However, in dreams and through prophetic words from trusted men and women of God, this word was made even more clear to me. Without knowing how we would do this, I said "yes."

At the beginning of this journey, I had questions, insecurities, and so many concerns. I was ashamed to ask these questions or to share how I was feeling.

I started in ministry at thirteen as a member of the praise team in my local church. Then I was given the opportunities to minister songs in special and Sunday services. I identified with this quite well. I was embracing the psalmist call and very excited about it. As time continued, I came into the role as mentor to many young women in my community. This journey would lead me to 2005 where I started hosting conferences and delving into my love to see many embrace the subject matter of true worship. This steered the course to begin ministering the word outside of my local church. I was excited and felt a sense of accomplishment right where I was in ministry. I did not have the slightest clue how to be a pastor, or how I would fulfill this call with my husband.

Experience would soon teach me that, all this time, I had placed so much emphasis on the preaching aspect of leadership in the church, but this was a small part of this call and assignment.

When 2012 arrived and I was faced with this new course—it was hard. I struggled with giving so much of my time. It seemed as if the hours in the day were not enough to return the calls, visit the homes, pray for those requesting prayer, and counsel those that needed advice. I was drowning.

One day, the Lord said to me that in order to be effective in this assignment, I cannot negate the natural requirements of my job.

As a prophet and pastor, I was becoming quite proficient in the spiritual aspect—ensuring that my sermons were well studied, laying on of hands, prophesying, assisting with praise and worship, ensuring the sound was stirring and conducive for God's presence.

This is what I was really good at. But the assignment required more. The people needed me to be more courteous, give a hug if needed, and sit with an individual to provide counseling. I learned that if this intimate system of checks and balances is neglected, my overall efforts as a pastor would be unbalanced and ineffective. At this point in ministry, the congregation was very small under twenty persons. I often wondered if I was the only pastor in the world being called upon by the congregants. Looking back, it makes me chuckle as I made mountains out of a single molehill.

I would be frustrated asking God, "What was the unique thing I carried that I was called to this?" This special thing that I was told every leader had seemed to not be the same with me.

Instead of answering my question directly, the Lord taught me lessons through my selfish behavior and limited thinking. These lessons were the beginning to my turnaround. I would like to share them with you.

# Take Unnecessary Walls Down

There was a little cozy bubble I floated in. However, my call required me to transform this into a massive ark of safety for everyone in our care. During this time, my husband and I would have occasional sit-downs with the covering for our ministry. Without ever saying a word, he would begin speaking about a plethora of subject matters.

He would share about being a servant unto God's people. He spoke about preparing for this phase of ministry and so much more. We sat for hours each time, gleaning from his wisdom. We knew he was speaking under the inspiration of the Lord. It was after those meetings that questions would be answered and strategy came into perspective.

My character was being built. The Lord taught me the importance of character development, being true to my word, being truthful at all times, and being a servant first. I had no idea why these lessons were necessary. This was becoming so challenging. I often wondered, "Is there anything else you have in stored for my life? Is there any more vacancies in the kingdom?"

At this stage, we were nearing the end of the first year of starting this new work. We were a small but growing congregation, and hands to help were few. So I decided I would take the initiative to clean the church for a few weeks. This would work out well because the alternative was to wait until a member got off from their traditional job to assist. Did I say a few weeks?

This became another arduous task for me. As weeks turned into months, I did not like the idea of me doing the cleaning. I would cry and complain to the Lord of how I am being mistreated, and I am believing that he would move on my behalf and rescue me.

One day, as I went through my routine of complaining, the Spirit of the Lord ministered to me so plainly. I heard, "Don't fail this course twice." I was startled and tried to figure out the meaning of this. Then I had an aha moment.

Five years earlier in my local church, the Lord had instructed me to begin assisting with the cleaning and upkeep of the church. But my schedule got so busy that this assignment was never carried out.

I still didn't quite understand everything, but it was that day my attitude changed. I started to clean and worship. I went over my sermons while preparing the sanctuary. I then began looking forward to cleaning the house of God. I even started liking it. I had a system worked out where I would complete even sooner. This chore became a leisure activity for me.

But just as I grew to love it, a young lady who had joined the church came to me one day and said, "I want to assist you with cleaning the church."

I told her over and over, "No, it's really okay."

She was so adamant about it. She showed up every week until one day, I allowed her to assist. From that day to the present, persons literally volunteer and insist that they want to clean the sanctuary.

This experience taught me so many lessons. Before this, I could not tell our membership about working and serving in the house of God in this way because I disobeyed the instructions initially given to me.

I learned that God will create ways to allow us to finish what we started or in some cases fail to start. He created ways for me to triumph in the present where I had failed in the past.

Many of the challenges we face as Christian leaders are not due to the tactics of Satan but a divine visitation of the Lord to prepare us as our name becomes greater and our territory is enlarged.

I strongly believe that there are times the Lord will not allow us to escape the uncomfortable, hurtful, and embarrassing moments, simply because he will allow them to serve a purpose in our lives.

Your job is crucial to the Body of Christ. So the Lord will remove you from comfortable environments and situations and prepare you for places of purpose. Because greater spaces and opportunities are inevitable, it is vital that the one sitting in the seat must have what it takes to lead effectively.

Once I made things less and less about me and more and more about God's will, things got easier. I didn't even realize when it actually happened, but I began to fall in love with being a pastor. I began to understand that my natural and spiritual responsibilities were a fundamental principle of pastoring. Therefore, being anointed and imbalance is a recipe for disaster and wasted time.

The walls I had built up that prohibited me from being a mother, a counselor, and a pastor to God's people were crumbling down.

When you have heard so much bad news and experienced so many disappointments, you can become programmed to believe that we should live in isolation and without trust. It becomes so much easier to believe the bad rather than the good. But God gave me some good news, and I want to share it with you

Everyone is not trying to hurt or betray you. There are some persons that believe in the anointing on your life, and they want to love you back.

# Embracing the Call Increases Responsibility

As pastors, we become engulfed in walking out of our office and mounting the platform, and everyone is eagerly waiting to hear what we will say. We express our individual preaching styles and watch persons be uplifted, healed, and even chastised.

But you will learn that in this call, the Lord will have you to preach in more ways than one. Sometimes, you won't speak to everyone at once, but other times, one by one, they will walk in your office and pour their lives out to you.

This phase of ministry challenged and stretched us even more. Embracing this call meant more responsibility. We were given opportunities to be more involved in the personal lives of the people we served. That's becoming acquainted with them outside of attending church or serving in a ministry area.

The more we grew to love this assignment, the more the members started trusting us. They trusted us with their secrets.

We had to be developed in our strategy of counsel. We read books and sat under teachings to enhance and make us even more ready in this area. We also set rules and regulations for ourselves. Some rules are as follows:

- Do not judge a person because of a moment, therefore learning which response is necessary in each moment.
- Be honest. Always tell the truth even if the one sharing is very close to us.
- Never speak just to be heard. If you don't have the answer, admitting that is always the best counsel.
- Being a trusted ear is just as important as being a trusted voice. Ensure we hear what is being shared with the right motives and intentions.
- We have no right to share intimate details relayed to us in confidence. This includes whether the person who shared the information made us angry or discontinued their membership with the ministry.
- Do not inflict fear for anyone to follow our counsel.

Leaders, you will also have moments where persons outside of your congregation will trust your counsel. Some of these times, they may share about their pastors. This is not an opportunity to grow your membership. Try to be as just as possible. If the issues appear salvageable, it's okay to express that. Do not allow greed to destroy a relationship that could be mended.

Just as persons trusted us with failures and embarrassing moments, they also made us a part of the triumphs. This required another level of responsibility as well.

As they shared payment increases, annual financials increase in their businesses, etc., we had to make sure we never made them feel responsible to do anything outside of what the Word of God said. Their money is their money, and whether they share it with us or not, we remain their pastors and committed to serve them.

# How to Handle Changing Relationships

A pastor will have to balance a multitude of relationships within the church. Some of these are their spouse, their children, their family members, the leadership or close working circle, the staff, the volunteers, the members (new and old), and the visitors. Along with the day-to-day relational aspects, the pastor must balance shifts and changes within these groupings.

Let's face it, things happen, and one situation can cause a relationship to change in an instant. Sometimes, we try to appear as if we are not affected by persons leaving our ministries. But we are.

In truth, whether someone attended for a month, two years, or ten years, there is something about our role that makes us think about our parishioners, regardless if we usually spoke often or not.

The reality is in our line of work, relationships often change. And change can be painful. In these moments, we must hold on to our peace and be determined to allow our actions to be an example of God's Word. If not, we will get angry, incite riots, and prolong the hurt we feel. People will leave. This is not always a negative thing. People have the right to make choices for their lives. And when they do, we must accept it sincerely and gracefully and move on.

In this portion of the book, I thought of some questions you may want some answers for.

How do I deal with a person who worked very close with me deciding to leave my ministry? People make this decision for various reasons. Based on their reason, you should plan effectively.

Below are five hypothetical reasons persons may leave their home church and some ways a pastor can deal with this departure:

1.  Strong offense

    When you learn of their decision, wait before you discuss with church's leadership. Try to evaluate this with a prayer and a prayer partner or a covering pastor. Even though you may be disappointed or even upset, try to find if there was anything done on your part to warrant the offense.

    Whatever your findings are, whether you felt it was your fault or not, a simple call or text can be very comforting (provided they are open to being contacted). Please thank them for their service and for their financial support. Pray a prayer of blessing over their new journey.

    Before this time, they were working and bringing your vision to pass. What they have contributed should always be appreciated.

2.  Associative departure

    This is when a close friend leaves a ministry and the other feels pressured or obligated to do the same. This is common. Some persons came to know of a ministry through that friend or loved one inviting them. Most times, these persons never found their purpose for being there. When that person leaves, they no longer feel connected.

    In this instance, please do the same as before. Reach out to provide any explanation needed and show love and support.

3.  A plateau was met

    Truthfully, no pastor wants to hear that any of their parishioners feel like they have stopped growing spiritually or have not grown during their tenure. Naturally, a pastor would attribute a departure for this reason to their own shortcomings in leadership.

This can be hurtful, but remember, they have the right to choose always. Respect their decision, and show your love and support through a warm embrace and prayer.

If this has happened a few times in your ministry, speak to your congregants, and find ways to learn if they are being fed spiritually.

4. "The Call of God"

Persons part of your congregation may express that the Lord has instructed them to branch out to start their own ministry. When this happens, please do not make this a long debate on who is ready and who is not. You can respond based on how this conversation came about.

I would like to share two scenarios with you:

1. They ask for a meeting. Share with you what they feel the Lord is saying, and ask for your thoughts on what they have shared. Not always but usually when they fall into this category, they are the ones open to counsel and even disagreement. This is still their choice, but provide time for training preparation right away.

   Whether you feel the time for them to move in this stead is soon or not, do your best to assist in this preparation and readiness program to the best of your ability: constructing a sermon, layout of funerals, weddings, christenings, counseling courses, administration courses, and dos and don'ts of an itinerate speaker, just to name a few.

2. Their approach is short and direct. They sit with you to make you aware of the plans they have already made. When this happens, even if they asked for your input, most times, the decision is made. It is quite possible that if

your thoughts or counsel disagree with their plans, they will not be receptive. If you are in disagreement, it will result in offense and a misunderstanding. But this may not be the same in all cases. Be led by the Holy Spirit.

3. Life transitions

There are three groups under the umbrella of this subtopic. These include persons who were wed and decided to attend the home church of their spouse. Most times, the female would be the one to transition to the husband's church, but some situations are different.

Pastors always remember they are a part of your family. Be there for both of them as much as you can, and encourage your church family to do the same.

Another is persons relocating for schooling or work purposes. Occasionally, your ministry may have a son or daughter venturing to another country or region for the purpose of pursuing a higher education or receiving a job offer.

During this time, make a special effort to keep in close contact with them, allowing them to know they are a part of your church family. Send video clips, and invite them to watch online services. Research worship centers in the area that share beliefs and core values. Contact their outreach personnel, and set up an introduction.

Lastly are persons who are not attending regularly due to old age or sickness. The elders of a church are the fountains of wisdom. They are pillars that keep us grounded. While this is so, the many effects of aging can prove problematic, affecting their ability to worship in person.

An occasional phone call or home visit will reassure them that they are loved by their church family. This group matters. We should always make the effort to express this.

# Manage the Season Called Few

For the most part, many environments that are a part of our culture teach us to prepare for "more." We hear so many admonishments and sentiments about increase. However, I learned a very valuable life lesson that we must plan and prepare for the times when we will have less than we desire.

Ministry is unpredictable. This uncertainty sometimes causes anxious behavior. All pastors desire growth and assistance to further the work we have been called to do. The intricacies of the season of few can either prepare you for more or cause you to crumble right where you are.

In this instance, we will surround the idea of "few" around church membership growth. Sometimes, there are long periods where growth is static. (Persons are not showing interest in joining the membership.)

Sometimes, despite not showing interest in membership, persons are visiting. Do not overthink these times. Do not pressure persons to become members or become angered if they visit other churches.

People have the right to visit and not become members of any church. Therefore, it is their choice of how connected they will be. They may give offerings but never become tithers. Do not make it about you. It may be due to personal matters that they are working out in their own lives.

Sometimes, young ministries make this mistake. We simply expect too much too soon. Having made this mistake ourselves, we want to help other leaders to avoid this or recognize this in their actions.

Here are six types of persons visiting your ministry:

1. Long-term visitor

    These persons have been without a church home for over a year and have become quite comfortable. It is possible that they were a part of their previous church home for several years. Severing ties from a long tenure could result in waiting a long time to officially connect again elsewhere.

2. Episodic visitor

    This individual pops in and out. They love the ministry, but their attendance is not consistent. This can be due to being an active member of another ministry or having obligations such as work or school.

3. Supporting visitor

    These persons have visited the ministry for over a year. They feel like family. They give and even assist wherever they can. Sometimes, they are actively a part of another ministry.

4. Transitional visitor

    Sometimes, a person is visiting a ministry since they are in a challenging place with their current ministry. They are in the process of making the decision to leave the membership. There are times transitional visitors are those that feel the call of God to embrace pastoral leadership, and your ministry is a place that is providing growth and preparation for them.

5. Parasitic visitor

    These are persons who are visiting for a self-serving reason.

6. Potential dweller

    These persons have a genuine desire to be a part of the ministry. They sow their seeds and serve however they can. They are focused and observant.

As pastors, we must pay close attention to the differences. Love everyone the same. But adding pressure and obligation too soon can cause a potentially beautiful connection or friendship to be destroyed.

It's laborious when you don't have adequate resources to do what is needed. But being anxious won't meet the need.

Strive to be responsible and integral, and in due time, you will have more than enough. While you are experiencing this time, find comfort in knowing it will not last forever. While you wait on the membership to grow, work to improve your brand as a ministry in any way you can.

# Manage Your Increase

*Increase* can be defined as becoming greater in size, amount, or degree. Increase is a powerful grace that shows up in our lives in so many ways. It is simply experiencing more in particular areas. Please know increase requires a manager.

In your time of few, God teaches you to be a manager of more by showing you how to be faithful over little. This is a profound principle that is used to ensure that more lasts in our life.

Be careful not to overlook your increase because it did not show up the way you desired. At one point, our ministry experienced a time where membership numbers were not growing. In the midst of this time, persons were moving on to be a part of other church families.

This time was challenging. I started seeking the Lord in prayer, asking diligently that the Lord would increase our numbers. I became so depressed as the thought of "there has been no increase in our ministry" started to overwhelm me.

One day, the Lord reminded me that more than half of the membership attends prayer meetings. I was a little taken aback as I did not consider this as a kind of increase. But as I sat and gave careful thought, I had to agree that it was.

I began to learn that we must celebrate every instance of increase because it matters and it serves a great purpose within our assignment. Every increase is needed.

I also took notice that the Lord began to expand my capacity to teach his Word. I gained perspective on relating to different audiences. This was an area I had struggled in before. At this point, people started to call in, saying that the Word is being preached with revelation and simplicity at the same time. Therefore, this was increase.

Persons part of the laity and leadership began growing in the "Things of God." They were finding purpose, showing greater responsibility for the roles within the church. This was increase.

Persons within the ministry took the initiative to pray for the pastor and working teams within the ministry would sometimes request to spend the night at the church, covering us and consecrating themselves for service to God. This was increase!

There was a more tangible experience of God's presence when we gather. More testimonies were being shared. This was increase.

Persons were receiving salvation in our service more than before. This was increase. We must look for the signs of increase around us and within us.

## Plan and Strategize

Plan for the things you are praying for. Are you ready to receive the answer to your prayer?

If you have served twenty-five persons in your congregation and if the number increases to sixty-five. It will require you to adjust your service to accommodate adequately. If there is no sufficient accommodation, you will see a short-lived increase.

For example, thirty-five chairs worked perfectly for the twenty-five. But it will not be sufficient for sixty-five. Adjust and make room for more. Therefore, in your time of little plan ahead, purchase seating each quarter. Doing it this way allows you to save toward this goal and prepare to store before they arrive.

Prepare to increase your diversity. Increase for your congregation may also mean different generation coexisting together. Learn ways to effectively and smoothly mesh relatable activities in one service.

More can mean updating and reequipping staff and volunteers to effectively serve a larger crowd or a different crowd than what they have grown accustomed.

Every increase in a season requires your protection for it to remain in the upcoming season. Therefore, prepare, plan, and strategize for every area that is changing in your ministry.

Sometimes, this preparation and strategy call for an updated understanding of what has increased in our season. Sometimes increase does not come in the form of larger numbers as adding bodies to the seats. It can also come in the form of,  the few that remain produces everything the vision needs.

While typing this portion, I felt strongly that there will be leaders reading this book that when you come to this part, it will feel unrelatable because you don't feel you have had an increase in a long time. I can hear you feeling and saying that you have done all you can, and still, you have seen no increase.

Well, pastor, my response to you is, "Sometimes, the increase is in the loss." What God allowed to remain is so much more than you see. God will show you he can do great things with what's left!

# It's Okay to Be Human

As stated earlier, many people see us pastors as superheroes with ultimate strength. Sometimes, for our own misguided reasons, we do not want to ruin their vision of us, so we try to appear this way. Please take this advice. *Ruin the superhero image by letting them know you are human.*

Please also note that in no way I am asking you to lower the standards of the Word of God. But simply, let your parishioners know you have imperfect moments like everyone else.

It's okay to rest. Take a break when you need to. Cry when you need to. Give an apology when you were wrong. And seek counsel when you are at a crossroad.

I had to be human enough to relay when a good idea was a thought and not a word from God.

As a prophet, I had to be especially mindful of this. As persons become acquainted with this aspect of my ministry and experienced the Word of God coming to pass, it became easy for them to equate everything I said as an instruction from the Lord.

One day, a few of my spiritual daughters and I were at the church. We were sharing about a myriad of things. I told one of them, "I would like to see you in this kind of car." We all agreed, laughed, and moved on in the conversation.

A few days later, I received a message from her stating to give my thoughts on her receiving a loan because she does not have the funds to purchase the car outright.

I was perplexed by this and asked, "Why are you doing this?"

She said, "The Lord wants me to drive a certain kind of car."

I then explained, "No."

That was my own thought and not the instructions of God.

I had to be human enough to receive ministry from another.

Pastors, many times, the answer we need and the refreshing we need will come through another. Many times, they will come from the laity in our ministry. Allow the people to bless your life as God has used you to bless theirs.

# Do Not Use the Microphone as a Weapon

One of our responsibilities is to preach the Word of God, providing atmospheres of cultivation, examination, and learning.

Therefore, we must hold this responsibility to a high order and be cautious with how this is carried out every time. As pastors, it is easy to clear our conscience in an environment where we are on the loudspeakers and others are not given room to defend or share their own sentiments.

I believe that our worship services are not the time to throw comments and opinions about matters personal to you because you failed to deal with them face-to-face where others will know your position or are able to rebut.

Keep sacred things sacred. The microphone is a tool in our hands to expand our voice as we teach God's Word. Handle it and the sacred desk as such.

# The Pastors Will Not Be the Only One to Bless the Membership

Our congregation is filled with people from different backgrounds, beliefs, and origins. Some of them will visit other ministries, while others will not. It does not make the ones who do disloyal.

Just as persons visit our services from other churches, we all should expect the same. As we come to the close of this first chapter, please remember that despite all the bumps and hardships, there will be lifts and easier times.

I pulled a few points from this chapter that I hope will remain with you.

- Prepare for everything you are praying for.
- Always look for the lesson in the hardship.
- Learn why God has called you specifically to this task.
- Preaching is only a small part of this job.

It is okay to accept you are human and not a superhero. "You cannot do everything." You have what it takes to be successful at this job. Even when you are uncertain, God's Word over your assignment is yea and amen.

C H A P T E R  3

# Uncertainty

As I began preparing for this, the third chapter, I felt it was pertinent to provide a current and relevant word for leaders who may be struggling with uncertainty. If you have ever been called by God to do anything, this is a word you will come to know oh so well.

"Uncertainty" can make a leader feel quite inept. Questions begin to swirl around in your mind like "How to express that?" "I don't have the answer for this or that." "How can I say God speaks to me?" And "I don't have a clue what to do about this." I have been here so many times.

*Uncertainty* is defined as being unsure of something. The matters can range from a decision with the ministry to a sensitive situation in your home, and the list goes on. When we as leaders find ourselves in this place, we must ensure that our focus remains on the vision God has given us. Do not become careless to things you are certain of because you have grown impatient waiting on the confirmations to the things you are uncertain of.

I must admit I was the cause of so many of the emotional ups and downs during seasons like this. When you have made up in your mind what the answer should be, one becomes quite unreceptive to any other possibilities. My times of being uncertain about what to do, who to reach out to, and which way to go on a matter taught me valuable lessons.

One of those lessons was don't be so consumed in the question that you don't listen to the answer. Let's explore this. Many times, the answer shows up, but our own desires and prideful intentions rob our seasons of its benefits because we decided what we wanted the answer to be or how we want it to come. When this happens, we place our future and the critical present moments of our lives in danger.

For example, if you are believing God for a mate, he places someone in your way who is kind, caring, respectful, etc. They express their interest to you, but they don't fit the criteria of what you expected.

Sometimes, in this case, your reasons are superficial. He/she is not the right height, weight, etc. So you overlook them and continue asking for a mate. So as time goes on, you become impatient because the time of when you will become married is unknown.

Another example is you were invited to join a fellowship. You want the Lord to instruct you about this on whether to do so or not. You are waiting for a dream or for a prophet to bring you the answer. However, you have spent time with leaders in the organization and have seen unintegral actions and malicious behaviors toward others.

Can you see how the answers came? Many times, the Lord answers us in these ways, but we simply overlook it.

As mentioned earlier, when we overlook God's answers, we wait in a place/season longer than God intended. This can affect our future because a time delayed in the now causes you to get to the next later. This also affects the pivotal moments in our current season as we miss opportunities for spaces and connections that were divinely orchestrated by God.

In other words, sometimes, your blessings depend on you arriving on time. There were some blessings and moments of favor you received later than intended because of your lateness.

As a leader who have been called by God for this time, please don't make the mistake to believe that the only thing you need to be blessed and favored is the gifts you possess.

It is the gift that causes you to perform despite your emotional and mental state. However, it takes obedience and accountability in each season of your life to keep you on schedule and eligible for the favor that comes with your season.

Times of uncertainty and waiting may sound simple to the ears of one who hasn't been here *yet*. We all will have our time to explore the uncertain place. Please believe that if a season like this is not handled and maneuvered through with patience and wisdom, it can wreak havoc in the life of an anointed man or woman of God.

> Then Jezebel sent a messenger unto Elijah, saying, so let the Gods do to me, and more also, If I don't make Thy life as one of them by tomorrow this time. Elijah was afraid and ran for his life. (1 Kings 19:2–3 KJV)

In this portion of Scripture, we have a man who was not just anointed but sent on an assignment by God.

This specific account began from the seventeenth chapter, when Elijah gave the prophetic release, "There will be no more rain." After this, he waited in the wilderness for three years. After this time, the Lord sent him back to the place and to the people whom he had released this word to.

When he arrived, he got to work, and there were several great victories in one day. God answered by fire. The people repented. There was an abundance of rain. The Spirit of the Lord rested on Elijah, and he outran the rain. It was a great day for the prophet, probably the greatest day of his life.

Then he got a message from Jezebel, stating she will take his life in twenty-four hours. This man of God became afraid and ran.

It's overwhelming when your great season doesn't last long. The memory of the false prophets being destroyed, the cries of surrender from the people that anticipated rain falling, and the wind that blew on his back while he outran the rain and the chariots, all must have still been fresh in his mind!

So how do you go from rejoicing to running in fear? Uncertainty! As a leader, you have some great days where God is moving in your life, and you feel fit for the call and excited about what God will do next. Then a diagnosis rattles you to the core, a divorce affects you mentally to the point you cannot recognize who you are, or a split in the church makes you uncertain of whether your life's work and ministry will be restored.

Situations like this shake the pillars in your life. It upsets your most intimate circles. It can cause you to become enemies to whom you once loved as sons and daughters. Times like this can cause you to question whether you are on the right course! It rattles the same faith you preached about and encouraged others to have.

Uncertainty can cause you to lose control. When this happens, it can cause us to lose credibility with those we serve.

It can cause us to make long-term decisions for a temporary misfortune or happening. Just like Elijah, many have made spontaneous decisions in such moments. Without seeking counsel or conferring with God, these kinds of decisions will cause ramifications.

# When Uncertainty Causes You to Lose Control

There is a normal and unhealthy form of uncertainty. The truth is we all will experience this throughout our lives. It's a part of the growth process. As we accomplish and journey to new levels of life and ministry, there will be many things we are not sure of. This can make us a little impatient. But this is typical.

However, when these times cause us to exhibit reckless behaviors and make dangerous decisions, this is the unhealthy form. I have given it a terminology to assist me with providing perspective for what happens in these times: "crazed uncertainty" When your uncertainty climbs to this level, there will be adverse effects. Earlier, I mentioned a few scenarios that can cause this to happen. Let's delve a little deeper into them.

When things in your life go amiss, you will learn how submitted and stable you are to the will of God. During these times, we see a side of us that we didn't know was there, or we thought was gone.

Many times, before the inimical responses, there are signs that show you are moving to close to the edge. These signs are the unobtrusive disorderly actions: snapping by raising your voice without cause, speaking condescendingly to those you lead, overreacting, silently feeling that a word the Lord spoke over your life is untrue and won't come to pass, not keeping your word, being irresponsible to personal prayer and study times, blatantly disobeying an instruction given by God or the counsel of trusted leaders.

These are all signs that you are losing control. If not corrected, you will go too far. When you find yourself here, be truthful about it.

Something is wrong. You need to *stabilize your emotions* so that you can continue in your God-given assignment.

Stabilize your emotion. Wow! To some reading this, it sounds like a medical term that should be used in the company of doctors, not pastors. However, I am learning that we have the power to stabilize our emotions. The emotion is a strong feeling deriving from one's circumstances or mood.

When I found myself in this place, there were a few things I did to reel me back in. I would like to share them with you.

Always keep up-to-date with all that God spoke about your current season. Please don't be too busy to document the dreams, the prophetic words from prophets and vessels you know are authentic, and the prophetic words the Lord spoke to you personally.

Recite them often to build your faith and be close to your remembrance. If you will make it to the greater season *sane* and *saved*, you must get there depending, believing, and remembering the promises God made to you.

Often times, the same words we preach and reiterate to the members of our church or to the followers on our live broadcasts are the same words and instruction we ourselves don't follow. We must hold fast to his word before the trial comes so that when it does, our *foundation remains strong.*

# Always Have a Check Person/s

In recent times, I have seen the reverence and acceptance for ministry covering decline. The term "covering" simply means a trusted individual/s that you can be accountable to and that will correct, encourage, and mentor a pastor/leader.

There are also people assigned to your life by God that may or may not have a title but have become voices in your life that you can trust because they will tell you the truth. Having these levels of relationship is beneficial to A leader. It creates balance and provides unbiased perspective on pivotal matters.

Hence, these relationships can be a shield in reckless times. Having these relationships is not enough. Obeying the counsel, respecting the rebuke, and embracing the fellowship are what makes these relationships add value to our lives and ministry.

# *The Aftermath*

I don't know the details of your circumstance. I don't know what mistakes you have made and how bad things look for you right now. Let's face it at some point. We all will find ourselves in this place: the aftermath of reckless behaviors and dangerous decisions.

The aftermath looks ugly. It resembles a bombed site with rubble (broken-down structures), smoke, and injured individuals everywhere. That's what we do when we lose control as leaders.

## We Break Down Structures

The structures are symbolic to the intangible things that are so vital to the growth of a ministry. Some of those are wise counsel, unity, integrity, stability in faith, and fellowship, to name a powerful few. You are an embodiment of grace and favor in the earth. As you stand and speak to God's people, your teachings and decrees and inspiring words through the grace of God, prepare them, propel them, and strengthen them.

When you are unstable, you put all of this in jeopardy. The secrets and frailties of them that trusted you are in jeopardy. Where there was a vibrant house striving to experience glory and prepare God's people, we now have rubble.

## Injured Persons

This is symbolic to mishandling people, taking advantage of their kindness because they would do anything for you, or involving them in a matter they are not grown enough to handle. It taints their view at the kingdom of God.

Many of them leave the church and stray away from their relationship with the Heavenly Father, not because they don't love you or don't want to serve God. They were not grown enough to learn about what another leader did to you or for you to break confidence and tell them the secrets that another leader or member shared with you.

If you are a single leader/pastor, an uncertain time can cause you to marry the wrong person. Your sons and daughters will become privy to the ins and outs of this reckless decision. If you are married and your marriage is falling apart, this is challenging, not just for the ones in the marriage but for them who were once blessed by this union.

It harms them. It injures their emotions and their mental capacity. Do not bring them into your chaos. Do not make them choose between their spiritual father and mother. It will injure their spirit. It can send them back to a place that God used *you* to pull them out of. Hence, this behavior can inflict cycles in the lives of people that are around us.

When we think of injuring someone, we often reflect on harming physically or verbally. However, this also includes forcing people to go beyond their emotional capacities. Among leaders, divorces happen. I'm sure this is a dreadful experience. This portion of the book is not written to judge your relationship or to take sides but to suggest that if these ordeals take place, let's ensure that we handle it sensitively and wisely, especially in the presence of those we are called to lead.

## Smoke

This is symbolic to how far our recklessness reaches. Please don't think you are only required to be integral and stable for the persons in your church. There are persons that you have never met in the natural world, but they have met your gift and your ministry. Something you said or posted on social media impacted them in some way. Now, they are watching you and consider you as a voice they can glean from.

When you made that reckless decision, it was like smoke. It was like impure vapor traveling beyond your ministry location perhaps beyond the country you live in. Therefore, when we make the decision to introduce our ministries to broader audiences, we must ensure that everything we do is done with them in mind.

I understand that leaders should be able to live their lives without the pressures and permission of those they minister to. When you say yes to the call of ministry, you are required to be responsible for the yes you gave.

Ministry requires responsibility and accountability. Though sometimes used interchangeably due to the closeness in meanings, these words possess a slight difference:

- Responsibility: The moral obligation to behave correctly
- Accountability: The acceptance of one's actions

# CHAPTER 4

# Ministry Fatigue

I'm sure this heading sounds like a cliché. But I admonish you to carefully and truthfully consider this.

How consistent is your prayer life as a pastor or leader, not the prayer you pray on service days for those who answer an alter call or those who call us throughout the day requesting prayer. That is one aspect of a prayer life. I am referring to the prayer life that sustains *your* life.

We as leaders are always giving and pouring out of ourselves. We do this through the preached word, counselling, and prophetic release, and the list goes on. Over time, carrying out the duties associated with our call, without prayer, can cause a gifted leader to become empty.

This kind of emptiness is identified by many feelings. More specifically, it can be a feeling of having nothing more to give, wrestling with the call that you once loved, struggling to minister with usual strength or capacity, or having a heavy feeling while ministering. The question is, when this happens, what is needed? The leader needs to be refueled.

Several weeks ago, I pulled up to the gas station. While I was there, I was told by one of the attendants that service would take a few minutes longer because the pumps were being refueled. I sat and watched as a huge truck pulled up to an area where a space in the ground had been opened up. A hose went down inside replenishing the gas.

In that moment, I realized that I hadn't thought about this before. That gas station fuels thousands of cars. Some cars receive a little. Others receive a full up. It appears to us that there is a never-ending supply. But as those pumps give, there is an allotted time they must be replenished. If this does not take place, the tanks will go empty, and vehicles can no longer receive from that provider.

This is the same with us as leaders. People believe that we ourselves never feel empty after continuously pouring out. This is not only referring to providing individual prophetic releases or laying on of hands. To stand up and preach a word that challenges and stirs the hearers can be draining to the ministering vessel.

# Praying Pastors

Dear leader, you must be replenished so that you can continue giving. How does this happen? We are refueled through our prayer lives and anointed atmospheres. Our refreshing is our own responsibility. When we neglect this essential requirement, we are not living up to our responsibility.

Ensure that priority is given to prayer and times of meditation. Ensure that you spend time in rooms where revelation is preached and the presence of God is felt. Find places you feel safe to receive.

Many of us have gone through seasons where we've had a preaching life but no prayer life. We have become handicapped by the cheering of the crowds. So our prayer times are mostly in front of a camera or with a cheering section. We struggle to pray when no one is around to clap and cheer.

I learned that there are some conversations that the Lord does not have in public. Thus until we commit to personal prayer, there are some information we will never come to know and some impartations we will never receive.

Though embarrassing to admit, I have struggled with my prayer life. There were some mornings I simply didn't want to wake up to pray and many that I didn't. There were times I set for prayer and I arrived dawdling. I found myself so busy with the church that I could not find time for God.

When you lack intimate time with God, you may be full of gift but empty of strength and peace. When a leader is in this state and continues to function, the emptiness causes extreme fatigue.

Here is the difference. To be empty is to function without a current encounter of God's presence on your life. The gift is a powerful resource in the life of a leader, and though the leader can feel the absence of the encounter, the audience usually cannot.

We can prophesy and lay hands in a powerful way without presence. However, over time, this emptiness causes extreme tiredness. There is more pressure on the leader's physical body to carry out a supernatural assignment without consistent God encounters. The gift alone is not enough for the vessel to remain at its best.

For example, a pilot who has been in the air, for many hours, taking passengers to different cities in record time, is doing their job well. However, that same pilot who has the knowledge and/or the gift to uniquely function even in pressurized circumstances will place every life in danger without proper rest.

A pilot that is tired and falls asleep while landing the aircraft is still talented and still knows how to do the job. But their skill can only function as great as the pilot can in any given moment.

An empty leader is dangerous to their assignment. Prayer and meditation on the Word fill you with resources for the days and seasons ahead.

When the gift functions within a tired and empty vessel, the level of what is produced will be drastically effected. Not only the God encounter releases anointing/power, but also that anointing is the approval for a greater level of function every time.

This greater level may not always result in individual prophetic words or demons being casted out in a service, but sometimes, it comes in the form of an evident presence of God Almighty, gifts stirring up and hearts being restored.

Absence of a consistent prayer life diminishes one's capacity to handle pressures that come with the call and even everyday life. As you face disappointments, loss, and pain while being in this state, it pushes you closer to the edge.

Pastors/leaders, there are times you must turn the cameras off and invest time in the presence of God so that you can maintain the strength that you need to function in your call.

While sitting and typing this portion of the book, the Holy Spirit said, "Tell them that another way to indicate that you are too close to the edge is when you quit being curious about ME."

Leaders, don't lose that. The desire to know everything you can about God, about his Word, and about his systems operating among us and in the heavens. I am a firm believer that good curiosity is the prerequisite for God clarity.

I was introduced to prayer through my grandmother who would literally talk to God in the morning, noonday, and night. I knew that I wanted to become versed in prayer, but I wasn't sure how to. This curiosity would take me on a twenty-five-year journey to date.

Growing up, I was of the persuasion that personal prayer time is a moment of talking to the Lord. However, as my relationship with the Lord strengthened, I learned that prayer time was so much more. One of the ways I can describe it is "It is a moment carved out for me to receive what I need."

I coined a phrase called the "prayer streams." Prayer streams are a collective of different experiences and expressions used within your prayer moment. I started taking my Bible into my prayer time. This opened and stretched me into a new understanding of my prayer time.

Reading the Bible is a form of communicating with God. It is ingesting the Word and responding to it with faith. Hence, I started setting time to include reading the Word of God in my prayer time. This pushed me into another "new" experience.

I started sensing and hearing revelation of the Word. Then I needed a writing pad. When I started bringing a notepad to prayer, the more I wrote, the more the Holy Spirit spoke. I noticed a significant change when I began bringing these tools to prayer (Bible, notepad, and pen).

Up to this point, I had experienced the Lord adding to the moment and allowing me to experience more in this time.

Then I experienced what I believe to be a prophetic word called "reform." My prayer time was reformed. Once again, I was left to place language to this. The most suitable explanation I can give is, my prayer became my classroom. So much was happening in me. A new road was being cut and paved through this experience.

I started increasing the activities in my prayer time. If the Lord told me to study a topic, sermons were built and prepared in my prayer time. Every song or melody the Lord would give in a dream or during the day was perfected in my prayer times.

Books were written in my prayer time. *This book* was written during my prayer time. As I engaged all these different activities and made them one with my communication with the Lord, prayer was never the same.

Verbal prayer and communication were also given its own set time in these moments. My meeting place for prayer was transformed and given a name "groaning place," a seeking place and a command tower of declaration and decrees with a greater understanding. I learned that God names what he uses. Nothing remains nameless that will be used in the Earth!

A prayer life saved my life. This powerful resource and favor given to us by God have stabilized my emotions, regularized my thinking, and strengthened me for the days ahead.

Prayer is the place for planned parenthood in the kingdom. One cannot be a spiritual parent in the kingdom of God without prayer. It is in this place that one is trained to handle not just people but destinies.

We learn how to stay on course because when a leader loses control, those that receive from them are delayed. You may ask, "How can this be?" But a leader that is out of alignment, most times, has lost Godly focus.

This does not mean you're not focusing on good things. But it is critical to focus on *God* things. This doesn't mean you must spend numerous hours with those you lead or that you must have all the answers for them.

It means your assignment to them remains an expression of God's will in a season. You will preach God's will, correct according to God's will, and counsel according to God's will.

I learned that prayer gives me access to the resource center of God. God is not short on supply. I learned that as long as I commit to pray, the room or space will never be empty. God is always there. As I began to have a clearer understanding of the purpose of the prayer time, God added to my experience yet again. Leaders, I encourage you to protect your life with consistent prayer.

As I was learning the formula for stability, I had another revolutionizing experience.

Remember I told you my prayer time was also my class time. Well, it was. The Lord began asking me questions. It began with me feeling the words very strong within me (this was early on in my development). I realized later that that can be likened to my spirit receiving or hearing information.

At first, I didn't know what to do with it. The same words I would feel deep within me would manifest somehow in dreams or with someone asking me the same questions.

This was an adjustment. The first time the Lord asked me a question, it was simple but yet one of the most difficult. I waited two years before I responded. The question was, "What do you want?" I didn't know what to say. I was terrified to get it wrong. So I waited.

One may ask, "Why would God ask questions? Isn't he all-knowing?" Honestly, that was my first thought. I said, "This cannot be God speaking to me because it is not consistent with his nature." Well, I was wrong. It most certainly is *his nature*!

I have come to learn when God asks questions, it is to really provide awareness to us. Sometimes, we are unaware of what we would do unless we are faced with a situation or a question. Other times, it is to speak to the matters of our heart.

In 1 Kings 3:5–28 New International Version, this account tells us about a young king named Solomon. One night, he was at Gibeon, and in a dream, the Lord asked him a question, "What do you want?"

The story says he replied, "God grant me a discerning heart so that I can man the assignment you have given me." I believe in that moment, he became aware that the assignment God gave him was priority in his heart. I must admit that there are times you don't know an answer like this until you have been faced with a question like this.

Then, in Genesis 3:9, Adam had made a terrible mistake. He was following God's instruction until he was faced with joining Eve in disobeying God, which was to eat the fruit God forbade him to.

After this happened, God asked him a question, "Adam, where art thou?" God knew what had happened. He knew his geographical location. That was a rhetorical question for Adam to examine what he had done and the consequences.

I will share three more questions with you that the Holy Spirit asked me in recent times.

# Question 1

In 2016, the Lord asked me the question, "Can I trust you with the future?" I had no idea what this meant. I had never heard this question before. I had no idea how to translate it to make sense to my life at that time.

There would be times in dreams that I would be asked this same question. In prayer, I would sense that verbiage strongly in my spirit until I grew so weary I felt frustrated. My position was, it's obvious I have no idea what this means, *so just tell me.*

I decided to share this with my husband. When I did, he said to me, "I don't see the problem." He said, "Your answer to this question is obviously no, and you are to prideful to admit to God you don't have the answer." Obviously, God is trying to tell us something is coming in our future that we must be prepared for. This could be good or bad.

The next day, I went in prayer, and with a broken heart, I admitted I cannot be prepared because I didn't even know what this means. This realization caused me to cancel my days at the office and pull away with God.

This was a lesson to me. Sometimes as leaders, we can become *too busy to receive the answers to our own prayers.* I then started to go through my journals. I started to revisit some of my questions and letters to God, and I realized there was a season.

I kept asking God, "Are we ready for where you are taking us?" I didn't realize that this question was the beginning of God's answer to my very own questions. I had become so busy over time that I didn't remember that I was waiting on this answer.

Then the Lord responded to my answer by saying, "store FOOD." We had no idea *why* we were being told to store food, but we wanted to be obedient.

In 2018, the Lord asked me the question again, "Can I trust you with the future?" When this happened, we knew whatever was coming must be close. We began preparing our church, our family members, those who would listen on the social media platforms.

We began storing cases and cases of food. Our main goal was to store enough for the entire membership, for up to 2.5 months at least.

Then 2019 came, and there was a cataclysmic storm that effected two major islands in my country (the Bahamas). We began planning and even accepting additional donations to assist with food and clothing distribution to those who were affected. We were so elated that we were prepared for this time as we were certain this was the reason we were asked to store food.

Then after our initiatives to assist with this disaster, the Lord said to us again, in 2019, "STORE FOOD." We were a little shocked as we thought the major storm was the reason.

Without hesitation, we continued storing and preparing our church to store food for their individual household, and my husband stored food once again in the event the membership ran out.

At this time, so much was going on in our country as lives had been lost due to the storm. Families were displaced. It was truly a challenging time for the entire Bahamas.

Additionally, many of our citizens were seizing the opportunity to temporarily relocate to the United States as others tried to make the best of what was left of their lives at home. We felt a burden to cover those who stayed and those that relocated.

One day while in Prayer, the Lord spoke to me saying the following:

> The next storm will be a storm of the air.
> Tell those who have traveled due to the recent
> storm to return to the Bahamas before April. If

they wait, they will try to come home and will be prohibited. Store food.

We realized what was coming was truly a "never had before" experience, and we needed to be prepared. We released this word to our church and on social media platforms.

Pastor Simmons prepared a seven-phase plan for this time. It seemed so extreme. I must admit that as he and I would discuss these phases, I would be terrified at the thought of what could be headed our way.

The phases included a storage plan. In Phase 1, instructions were given to the membership to store, as able to do so, 2–3 cans per week out of grocery purchases and do not go into storage until they were given the word from God.

A time frame was given also of storing heavier, storing 5–6 cans with every grocery store visit and storing aggressively, storing as much food as possible. We were also instructed to ensure expiration dates were 2–3 years from purchase date.

This phase also included every household receiving a water filter in the event water was affected for any reason.

In Phase 2, we thought that if we have to store food, there is a possible food shortage, and if that is the case, we should begin planting and growing food.

We held meetings with our church, sharing any knowledge we had on planting and growing food. The ministers were ahead of the game. They all were planting and growing right away.

In Phase 3, we implemented a system to ensure no matter what, we are in touch with every person part of the membership. At this point, we had not shared all of what the Lord had said to us. We shared in parts as we were released.

Despite this, in 2019, the evangelism leader of our church expressed a keen interest in receiving updated information for all the members and followers of the church, ensuring that phone contacts and addresses were current. We had not shared with them the task the pastor was about to assign. As I saw this, my heart was filled with praise. As we were in tuned with God, our sons and daughters were moving in the vein of the Holy Spirit.

Shortly after, Pastor and I spoke with the evangelism leader, making her aware that we need her to provide each minister in our church with a list. By weekly, the lists will be swapped. But every week, they will call the persons on their list to ensure they are well.

We decided as time came close, we can implement the other parts of this plan. By the time 2020 came, the whole world as we knew it was forever changed due to a pandemic and so many other circumstances that came along with it.

Our preparation for this time came from a seven-word question. For the entire first year of the pandemic, I was in *awe*. As we never stood on the food lines, the members of our church and others were provided for if there was a need. We did not run out of food.

Every week, each member and follower received a call to find out if they were in need of groceries and if they were well and the like.

As pastors/leaders, we will be faced with managing first-time impressions. This pandemic was something we had never experienced individually or as a church family before. This would be the first time our church family would experience such a time of crises in their lifetimes. They got to see how their pastors managed this time though it was not by our own strength or intellectual understanding but by obeying the instructions of *God*.

I must admit I was truly shaken in my spirit as I knew that my own carelessness almost caused me to miss what God was saying. Pastors, we must not become so busy with church that we end up not being prepared for ministry.

# Can You Manage Greater influence?

This was a tough one. Here is how it happened. I was praying for our church. We were coming to the end of a year, and I was covering our upcoming year and decreeing favor and blessings with faith. During these times of prayer, one of the things I constantly prayed for was greater influence.

One day, I heard in my spirit clearly, "Can you handle more influence?" At that moment, I paused with a puzzled look as I never thought about it. To be honest, I had a basic idea of what it meant, but I didn't really have the full understanding.

That very moment, I got up and pulled up the *Webster's Dictionary* to see the official definition. *Influence* is defined as the capacity to have an effect on a character, development, or behavior of someone or something. When I read this, I said, "WOAH!" This is truly a powerful word that comes with a whole lot of responsibility.

It was in that moment the Lord reminded me about two situations. The first one was a family matter. I was not that vocal about it because I had made a decision to never associate or connect with those persons again. In my mind, it was a foregone conclusion.

The second was a situation that took place years ago. I didn't remember it because once again, I had made a decision that the persons associated with the situation no longer existed in my world or any other world.

In that moment, the Lord revealed to me that it's a dangerous thing to give someone influence who is merciless. Not only did I have unforgiveness, but also I was trying to justify my reason for harboring the bitterness in my heart. I sat there going back and forth, giving reasons why I should be angry.

For several days, that encounter rested on my heart like a brick wall until I came to truth and my will broke and I confessed that I was wrong.

Influence is a currency of heaven. It is a grace the Lord gives to one to change atmosphere elements and the hearts of men for the glory of God. If that grace is mishandled, many people who are unable to defend themselves will be disadvantaged. The Lord made it clear to me that godly influence is not entrusted to the proud and the disobedient.

# Are You as Good a Daughter as You Are a Mother?

While I type this section of the book, I can feel the same chills I felt when I was asked this by the Holy Spirit. Let me just tell you the whole truth! I struggled with adding this specific question in the book.

One of the reasons I obeyed the Holy Spirit and my husband to write this book is because I kept reflecting on how terrified I was when we were planning our first service as a church. When we received the flyer from the graphic artist and I saw it on social media platforms, I was terrified. As I kept asking, "How do I do this?" I don't know the first thing about being a pastor. I kept feeling I was bound to fail.

I kept looking for books that would answer some of the topics addressed in this book. I am not saying they are not out there, but I didn't find material that walked me through this phase. This was one of the questions I wanted someone to walk me through because the truth is, *my answer was a resounding no!*

From a very early age, my biological father was not closely involved in my daily life and upbringing. He was around, and I believe wholeheartedly he loved me as I loved him. As I got older, around the age of fourteen, I started spending more time with him.

Then there was my mom. She is the most amazing woman in the world and, in my eyes, by far the best mother one can ask for. However, most of my years growing up, she was ill. I would watch her still making us breakfast and washing our clothes, but that frown in her forehead gave it away that despite all she was doing, she was in pain.

I didn't even realize it, but around the age of ten, I started to become distant from my mother, in ways that I hugged less, said I love you less, and would spend less time around her.

The older I got, I was very protective of her, ensuring everything I could do and that she needed were done. Even though I loved her with my whole being and wanted to protect her, I tried not to show closeness. Here I was a young girl becoming quite comfortable with knowing my parents are there but not wanting closeness.

My grandmother continued to visit us even into my teens. She was so strong and appeared well, so I was okay with being close with her. I hugged and kissed her and wanted to be around her all the time.

One of those times together led me into a life-changing experience. One night, she took me to a tent meeting being held by a young but very powerful ministry, led by two of the greatest leaders, a husband-and-wife team. That night, I rededicated my life to the Lord and continued attending that church.

During this period, God graced my life by putting a few amazing men and women in my life, all of whom were incredible in every sense of the word. I met each of them at different stages of my life. They all brought something unique and needed to my development.

The church that I joined steered the course and began the process in developing me to be the wife, prophet, and pastor that I am today. It was in this place that I learned that I had worth and purpose.

My apostle would literally correct me in public and would likewise defend me publicly. I remember one day, while walking in his office, I was totally taken aback as he was in a conversation but stopped abruptly to say to the person he was speaking with, "Please work with Tammy. There is a serious call on her life."

He was never too busy to listen even when I had nothing noteworthy to say. He made it seem like what I had to talk about was the most important thing in the world.

Then there was my apostle's brother. He too was a father figure. He was the second to the last child of his family. He and his wife would visit my school to make sure I was maintaining mannerly behavior and completing assignments. He would ensure that my needs were met.

And boy, he was never afraid to raise his voice when I was out of line or acting inappropriately with boys. Whenever I was ill at school, if they could not get in contact with my mom, the school would call him.

Every boy I was interested in, he had to meet in person, and he made it clear that at the end of the eleventh grade, a boyfriend could be considered.

Then there were two great men that came into my life when I was about to graduate senior school.

One of my teachers at school invited me to their youth meeting. I started attending the youth meetings. I had no idea that this angel would be one God would use as a mother in Zion to save my life so many times.

The senior pastor gave us lessons on integrity and how to walk upright. It appears he saw everything, and as busy as he was, he knew what was going on in the life of every young person. His brother whom we affectionately referred to as Uncle became a mentor and a disciplinarian.

He and his wife was a part of God's master plan to nurture me into my destiny. It appeared their patience never ran out, and I can say I did try their patience. There was never a time I called and they did not answer with love and favor. They both handled me with love, firmness, and affirmation.

He had a way about him that when the youth heard his voice if we were thinking anything untoward, we began acting accordingly. He always took time to give me counsel and advice. He did it with such care and concern that every time *he* spoke, I made it my business to listen.

Then I grew older. I guess life happened. I got busy and carried away with ministry, marriage and life that I didn't find time to show appreciation or to fellowship. Honestly, it appears that it was always quite easy for me to love and appreciate persons but not publicly express it.

As I reflected on my relationship with my biological father, that's how it always was. With my mom, that's how it became.

There would be years that would go by, and me just knowing that they were okay was enough. I figured there is no need to do the extra stuff.

The Lord began to deal with me concerning this. Here I was being a spiritual mother and instructing, correcting, and expressing in this capacity but unwilling to express and receive in the capacity of a daughter.

We are in an era where spiritual parenting and its importance are being dishonored and discounted by many. I would watch persons publicly declare there is no such thing as a spiritual father or mother. I would be angered. As I began to carefully examine what the Lord was saying to me, I realized my actions meant the same even though it wasn't expressed the same way.

I submitted this before the Lord. I began to make steps to equal the playing field to be as good of a daughter as a spiritual mother.

There are so many theories and opinions on who is a father, who is a mentor, who is a spiritual instructor. I have come to narrow it down to this: If anyone has ever cared, given, prayed, and protected you in anyway, they are worthy of your honor, love, and fellowship.

# CHAPTER 5

# A Reintroduction of Oneself

I have come to accept that there are so many aspects of the preparation for our call. This will include changes, and alterations. One of the most notable changes in my life up to this point was when the Lord reintroduced me to *me*. The only introduction I was given was by my parents and senior folks in my life. They did a pretty good job, making me aware that I was special and was given a special purpose by God.

One of the first changes I encountered was accepting and acknowledging the call as a prophet. At age of eighteen, my life totally changed. I had a dream. In this dream, I was told you are a prophet. When I woke up, nothing appeared to be the same.

After this dream, a prophet confirmed this. And I was very confused. I was really comfortable with the psalmist call and didn't quite understand what to do at this point. However, I started going over different stages and experiences in my life, and this new information did somehow make sense.

At the age of thirteen, I started dreaming very accurately. At age of sixteen, I had a keen sense of discernment. At the time, I didn't know what it was. At the age of seventeen, there was the super-strange feelings of emotions *and* even pain that is still unexplainable to this day.

For instance, I would see someone that I knew, and all of a sudden, I would have strange pains, and if I mentioned it most times, the person would say they are having that pain as well. When they or I would leave, I would be back to normal again.

During this time, I met my husband. After we were dating for several months, I attempted so many times to share these experiences with him, but I thought he would believe I am out of my mind.

At the age of eighteen, I started having even more experiences. After the dream mentioned above, I started seeing people draped in colors and hearing names while persons would pass my vicinity. I thought I was going out of my mind.

I kept this as a secret. I dwindled into depression until my husband who was my significant other at the time kept probing, asking, "What is the matter?" I opened up and shared just a little. His eyes lit up with excitement. The look in his eyes caused me to keep sharing until I shared all that was happening with me.

His response was so confusing. I was relaying this while crying, and he was so excited and started speaking of the goodness of God.

He then said, "When you hear the names, do you ever ask the person if they know of that name?"

I said, "No." (I wondered, *What kind of question is that, and why in the world will I ask them such a thing?*)

He said, "Well, the next time it happens, that's what you should do."

I said, "While passing that lady on the bus stop, I heard a name (Bertha)."

He turned the vehicle around and drove back to the bus stop. We pulled in front of the lady, and I humbly asked, "Ma'am, can I ask you your name?"

She replied, "My name is Albertha, but I'm called Bertha."

I began shaking, wondering what to do next, while my significant other is laughing out loud and thanking God. I said in a frantic tone, "Let's go. Let's go."

I knew something had changed in my life. I wasn't the same. But I could not figure out what to do next.

I had the Word from God. I had the gift in operation, but there was so much more I needed to be ready to be used by God.

At this point, I was a postureless prophet. I loved God. Worship was like water to me. But I struggled with respect and honoring those who God had assigned to my life.

I will never forget a conversation with the late Ruthmae-Bonnie Miller. One of my greatest regrets is that I didn't have the opportunity to tell her thank you. In this conversation, she said, "God has anointed you to do great exploits. Don't allow your attitude and behavior to allow God to raise up another in your stead." There I was, "miss know-it-all," quite offended and unreceptive to one of the greatest pieces of advices I would ever receive.

This season was so hard. It seemed like nothing made sense. I became angry. I was angry for several reasons because my college plans had fallen through. Ministry was stuck. To make matters worse, I was instructed to leave my job. I left my job and waited for a set of instructions that never came until one year later. And those instructions were, go to the beach every day and pray.

One morning, as I was walking to the bus stop to begin this prayer assignment. I was thinking, *I need to find a seminar, a school, something to teach me how to be a prophet. Then maybe this ministry saga will make sense.* As I spoke those words within me, I heard a response that said, "You can find a seminar. You can find a school to teach you what they know, but you will always struggle with the prophetic call within you because you have dishonored the prophets assigned to you."

It was in that season that I learned that God relationships (spiritual parents, mentors, destiny helpers) operate as keys in the lives of the recipient. Their presence and impartations unlock the mysteries of our call and season.

Before this, my ministry responsibilities consisted of arriving to church on time and showing up for ministry team meetings on time. Most times, I struggled doing that at the very least.

After this introduction, I was given more responsibilities. At this time, I was instructed to wake up at two in the morning to pray then at midday go to a public beach for prayer every day. I was required to give a lot of apologies. I had never seen a season like this before.

The prophetic atmospheres I sat in always gave prophetic words with hard instructions. My dream patterns were directly instructing me and challenging me in ways that I had never been challenged before.

I was confused and frustrated. Then the Lord revealed to me in a dream: "I am giving you a disciplinary regiment that guarantees brokenness in my presence, purity, and the grace to deliver."

I had no idea what this fully meant, but two words stood out of the whole encounter—"disciplinary regiment."

I began on a journey of pruning. I couldn't go everywhere. I no longer felt it was acceptable to wear revealing clothing. I was required to study. I was required to pray. As the years progressed, I was pulled into the classroom with God. I was taught that the greatest assignment of the prophet is not to speak; it was to listen.

I learned that my gift was not enough for me to remain blessed. An anointing was required. This came through the approval of God. I was required to pass the tests of character training every season.

The Holy Spirit and I had hard conversations. One in particular, the Lord said, "A gift is on your life, but you are not ready for my word to be in your mouth because a lying tongue cannot be trusted to speak on behalf of the Father of truth."

It was through these conversations that my perspectives and entire life were being circumcised. My audiences were changing. I had to catch up to this place I was pulled into by my call.

In the year 2012, the Lord made me aware that I was entering into another new chapter. At this point, my husband and I were pastoring one year in. As I tried to obey the instructions of God, I focused on the finishing date of this classroom and embarrassing season. However, I soon realized that to be in the will of God would mean to agree to be a student for the rest of your life.

As time went on, I was able to learn that the purpose of this time is to introduce me to a grace that resides on the inside that I have no clue is there. Then train me to use the grace that has been revealed!

I had gone through this rigorous process after discovering I am a prophet. As I shared earlier in the book, I was quite shocked when I learned my husband and I would pastor

As I entered into pastoring, I could clearly see that my training as a prophet prepared me to embrace and succeed in this call. The reason I am sharing this particular experience at this point is because every phase of your life has a purpose and every experience and lesson learnt will somehow contribute to the days ahead in a great way. Enduring the process helped me to become ready for my new season.

C HAPTER 6

# Shifting Seasons

This heading reflects times in our lives where what we once knew or experience becomes different. Not only for a pastor but also for any human being, frequent changes are tiresome. Don't you agree? Season shifts can fall into three categories:

1.  Painful changes

    Even though breakups can fall in this category, I wanted to speak solely about losses through death. Whether it's a child, a spouse, a parent, or a parishioner at your church, you will never grow immune to the pain of this kind of loss. And adjusting to this presents its own pain.

    Another example is diagnosis that requires regular treatments. It adjusts your quality of life. Pastors are facing these kinds of changes every day. In the midst of it all, we are fulfilling our call.

2.  Euphoric changes

    These kinds of changes are the ones that make others envy you. It's unbelievable, and you are overjoyed it took place. This can be finally getting the home of your dreams, the job of your dreams, or even the opportunity to minister in a place others dream of.

63

3.  Stretching changes

Below, there are several examples for your review. Shifting is required in every season of our lives. With every new season, there will be a new experience. Therefore, we are also required to move with the times.

This movement is referring to not only a possible relocation but also a moving into a better version of yourself. To do this requires decisions, reality checks, admittances. These are all kinds of movements.

Sometimes, we are so busy preparing our congregation for their next that we fail to adhere to our own instruction. Therefore, we arrive to the new as our old selves. This may not seem like a problem, but this is why we leave a wealthy season *empty*.

We may not have been given the seed to fund the vison or many new members walking through the door, but somehow, God has designed the new time to put a *new* thing in your hand. If you didn't embrace or maximize that opportunity, this season of change will become strenuous when it could be a blessing.

Leaders, it's not enough to hear about what God is doing next. Are you prepared for your next? Are you evolving for the new that is ahead? This may require a degree, a savings plan, etc.

This is the kind of change that can be good or bad, but it requires a great deal from you. This kind of change is where one must rise to the occasion to receive its fullness.

Sometimes, this kind of shift come through redundancy or retirement. When you have done something for a significant amount of time, not doing it anymore will be a challenge. Career shifts can also come with a promotion, and one is faced with measuring up to all that is required of them or becoming comfortable with a new working community.

Sometimes, the dynamics of changes within your close circles can be very challenging. Some reasons this occurs are a friend moving away or the ending of a relationship or friendship. This is a traumatic experience. Whatever the reasons may be, you will miss your friend or loved one. It will require a change on your part as the season in your life continues.

Maybe your congregation has shifted, or your leadership team has changed. Pastors, it's okay if you feel stressed or even uncomfortable in these times. But don't allow this to delay your preparation and strategy.

C HAPTER 7

# Consecutive Storms

Pastors, I admonish you. The toughest part of this call will not be how you struggled to adjust in the beginning. But it will be that at some point you fell in love with your assignment, and when this happens, you can become unbalanced. In that you neglect your happiness, your family, and your needs for it.

The job will become pretty demanding. But when you arrive to this phase in the journey, stay focus. Do not allow the call to destroy your family and your overall well-being.

Our topic above has led us to this place. Oftentimes, these changes create storms in our lives. Many times, it's not just one challenging encounter, and many years later, another takes place. Sometimes, it's one thing after the next. Have you ever felt like you can barely catch your breath because something is always spinning out of control?

To some regular person who has a perfect life, these headings are simply phrases in a book, but to many of you that will read this book, these are real live truths that you are living and trying to cope with every day.

These kinds of changes are happening in our lives time after time, the loss of a loved one, relationships severing, and the list goes on. They affect the pastor in a great way.

Frequent changes create consecutive storms. You cannot determine a pastor's emotional state by just looking at them. Most times, you cannot determine it by a conversation either because pastors rarely share what's really going on. They rarely tell you that they are drowning in changes of their current season. This is not a typical conversation for a Holy Ghost-filled man or woman of God.

Truth is there haven't been safe places created for pastors to admit how they are really feeling sometimes.

Here are some things pastors want to say but feel they can't:

- I don't want to do this anymore.
- I am *not okay.*
- I *need a break.*
- I am scared *too.*
- I don't have the answer.
- *You have hurt me.*
- I feel like a failure.
- I feel alone.
- Sometimes, I just want to be a regular person.
- I have needs too.

As changes persist. The pastor in us becomes tired. This experience in ministry creates another kind of tiredness. It's different from the kind of tiredness that comes from time away from God's presence. This kind of tiredness is called *soul exhaustion.* This usually comes from being overworked or not replenishing from a highly stressed environment.

An article written in 2018 entitled "Power of Positivity" shared ten ways to know your soul is exhausted. I want to share them with you:

1. You wake up, and you don't feel rested.
2. You constantly daydream about living a different life.
3. Your body aches often.
4. You feel disconnected from life.
5. You have intense emotions that you cannot explain.
6. You frequently feel loneliness.
7. You suffer from anxiety, depression, or other mental illness.

8.  You dread going to work every day.
9.  It feels like you are on autopilot all the time.
10. You no longer feel joy in activities that once made you happy.

A pastor is more than a preacher a few days of the week. We are people that are in love with the vision God gave us to the point that it makes us reckless at times. We work and give beyond our emotional budgets.

Spending countless hours on the phone counselling, praying, and prophesying, go home, and start all over again—sometimes working with every functioning team in the church, ministering to local assignments, traveling, and ministering internationally.

Personally, I can attest to this and try to be there for my immediate family while undergoing health challenges. In the midst of all this, I try to be a good wife.

There I was a pastor who had not wanted to do this then fell in love with it. But I found myself falling out of love with ministry. I was contemplating quitting. I kept dwelling on the hurtful actions of people that always indicated my efforts were not enough. I was convincing myself that maybe this is not for me.

My days got darker. I struggled to sleep. I struggled to feel. It felt that everything stopped, but somehow, I was still going.

After months of feeling this horrible way, I spoke with my husband. His response to me was, "Baby, you're just tired. You barely sleep. You take on all the tasks that persons fail to do or complete. You're juggling all these hats while doing others jobs. You're tired." As I admitted to myself and my husband that I was depleted, I felt like a failure.

I neglected my home, my marriage, and me. And I could not give a confirmed answer whether it was worth it or not. I did not know if it was appreciated.

We hear so much about "church hurt." Usually, this term refers to pastoral leadership and how they have went wrong. Is there any posts, blogs, or books about the hurt and abuse pastors endure? Many are guilty of it. I was guilty of it as well.

I had wanted so much of my pastors, not considering their personal life and obligations. I have been quick to mention what they did not do and rarely mentioned what they did do.

I talked about how I needed this or that and didn't realize or took time to know if their spouse, biological children, or siblings were getting enough of them.

I didn't put value to the word being preached every week and the times of training they did give to me. Learning how this felt was devastating.

Pastors preach through the insults, whether discreet or blatant; the attitudes; the inconsistencies of those that should bear their hands up; the personal battles; and so much more.

There will come a time when all of this makes your soul tired. When you begin to feel this way, there is a good chance that you will feel alone and perhaps want to renege on the yes you gave God at the beginning of this journey.

Despite how you feel, you are not alone. I encourage you to find and acknowledge the people who sees your effort.

There is an amazing group of people that supports and appreciates your sacrifice and effort. They are the ones that will push the vison to the best of their ability. They will cover you when you are not at your best.

I have learned to appreciate these gifts in my life. There are persons that make a special effort to encourage. They remember to be there when it counts. Sometimes, it's a simple text message or a drop by at my office. Despite how heavy the pressure in this job becomes, their presence reminds me that there are people rooting for me to succeed, depending on my yes to the call. They appreciate every deposit made.

It is important to know that even in shifting seasons that make us deeply sad, God is still working. Additionally, take a moment, and receive this word for your own life. Most times, you're the one giving hope through direction to others, but take this moment.

Don't allow shifting seasons that made you sad to rob you of the new. There is more water in your belly to spring forth, and God is not through with your vision yet.

You have become so comfortable being someone's pastor that you neglected every other gift inside of you.

It is the plan of the enemy to rob you of the greater thing in *you*. When you face season shifts, there is a resource within you that you have not been introduced to before. Many times, you didn't open your heart and mind to receive it. Therefore, you came in a new season using old resources.

There are new revelations of the word, an upgrade of the prophetic power approved to flow through you. But you are stuck on a grade because *you* only preached to others about more and believed for more for those in your church. But you never sat and believed that there was more in *you*.

When your seasons change, you are required to flow with the new thing, whether it's a new circle, new mindset, exploring a new talent or gift.

If you are reading this and you are not the senior pastor of a church but you function in some leadership capacity whether in your home, work, community, or church, I hope what you have read assisted you with understanding your pastor. Senior pastors that are reading this book, I hope you have understood so far those unexplainable feelings in the pit of your stomach.

You are not crazy. You have not lost your anointing. But you must do what's necessary so that you can be okay again. Your soul is tired because you have neglected the greater *you*!

*You* smile sometimes, but you're not happy. You show up, but you're discouraged. You are still preaching, but the fire of your belief is going out. Chances are, pastor, you are not happy.

What else is in there waiting to come out? What other gifts have you discovered in your treasure lately?

When your prayer life is intact and your ministering powerfully but you are still not happy and fulfilled, you are overdue for discovering another part of you.

Soul exhaustion can be healed through new goals, discoveries, and rest. The Lord wants to release this answer to your agony,

Read the next part slowly. Then read it again. Rest is *your* recuperation and discovery strategy. *You need a vacation* (stop putting off the vacation). You don't have to travel, but you need to carve out times where you focus on you and your household:

- Diet. Eat balanced meal. Eat on time. Quit going all day without a meal because you're "busy."
- Express how you feel, and focus on your needs. Set realistic daily goals. Don't add too many responsibilities for one day. If you're sad, that's okay. If you don't want to be bothered, that's okay. If you are sleepy, go to sleep. If you are hungry, *eat*.
- Don't allow the expectations of people to be the bar you set to determine whether you are a good leader. Some people will never consider your efforts as enough. The more you try to be enough, they will find more reasons to complain, and you won't be able to fulfill your assignment to the next person.
- Do something for you. Go to lunch, have a spa day, or do nothing at all. Take time to learn more about an area you are struggling in. Allow yourself to be ministered to for a change.

Here are some daily acknowledgments that I would say to myself until it became a part of my new strategy. You are encouraged to do the same. Here goes:

- I am not blaming myself for anything that is beyond my control.
- My best is always good enough even if someone didn't feel it was.
- My sincere apologies are good enough even if someone else don't want to accept it.
- I am not inept if I say no to anything that I feel will push me over my emotional limits at a particular time.
- I am not irresponsible if I consider the needs of myself and my household above nonurgent matters.

- I am not less of a pastor and prophet if I don't have all the answers.
- I am still anointed even if I am not feeling my best some days.
- It is okay for me to be human, have days off, engage in recreational activities.
- Admitting I am in pain is heroic and not cowardly.
- Accepting help and counsel from trusted voices and ears is a kingdom culture.
- I will not lose control.

I love my job. I love all those that I serve. I am ecstatic about the *new*—a note to those working in leadership or working a role in your local church.

I firmly believe that there is a group of people that is graced and anointed by God to assist in the carrying out of a vision given to a set of man and woman of God. These people possess the unique ability to provide the missing piece to aid its coming to pass.

These gifts are not limited to any one or two sets of people and callings but rather a diverse group, some of which you have not met as of yet. I believe that each vision will be assigned different gifts just as one mandate differs from the next. What one needs differs from the next.

First Corinthians 12:28 is a profound account in Scripture that highlights a structure within the church. It talks about apostles, prophets, miracles, and healings, and this is powerful. I love reading this part. But two graces were also mentioned—helps and administrations. These are those that work and those that lead in some capacity. Though often overlooked, it should not be taken for granted.

I urge you not to take your current role in your church or your call to operate this way in the kingdom for granted. Some persons are anointed by God to be the wind in the sail of the ship. Though the wind is not seen, its presence is felt, and its purpose cannot be denied. Without it, there would be no movement.

Leaders and workers, ministry can be tumultuous. Some of you get to witness firsthand the shifting seasons and even the moments that leaders lose control.

I would like to share two points:

- Point 1

I have seen so many times the working of the devil to destroy these relationships. One of the ways this plan is successful is through silence—conversations that need to be had but isn't.

Please, in all your work, develop balance—a balanced life in and outside of ministry. Balance your role. Seek God for instructions in every new season so that you are not just working, you are producing.

If you are drained, please make this known to your leaders. You may need a short break. If you are offended, make this known to your leaders. You may just need a heart-to-heart talk.

If you feel unappreciated, though it can get awkward, please share your feelings. The enemy wants to taint the intentions of your leaders. There may be an explanation for what is happening.

You are needed, not just by your church and your pastors but by yourself and your family. You are the difference in your local church, and your role is super important.

- Point 2

You are an armor-bearer to your senior leaders. I know. I know. The traditional definition of such a person is one who carries the Bible, etc. Hear the revelation of the Lord. Everyone that holds up the hand of their leader through service, prayer, and sowing of seeds, you are an armor-bearer of the set man or woman of God.

I urge you to do just that. In order to do that, self-examine your commitment. If you are serving on the praise team, protocol team, intercessory team, etc., you are lifting up their hands. You are making a burden lighter. Therefore, work toward the vision, and do the best you can to fulfill your assignment.

# *Pray This Prayer with Me, Pastor*

Dear God, please don't allow the pressures of this job to rob me of happiness.

Don't allow me to die from stress and worry before my time. I pray for loyal friends to have great laughs with.

May I always have a safe place to express my truth in hard life moments.

Introduce me to the greater me in every season of my life.

Introduce me to people that have the answers or solutions, those in and out of the church.

Strengthen and replenish those that work with us closely daily. Daily, load their lives with benefits.

May my love continue to increase for you. May you hear my voice every day not only in conversations with others but also in conversations I initiate with you.

My answer is still yes.

Amen.